Where Do Balloons Go?

and other poems

Where Do Balloons Go?

and other poems

by

Lexy Higgins

Appletree Press

First published in 2006 by

Appletree Press Ltd
The Old Potato Station
14 Howard Street South
Belfast
BT7 1AP

Tel: +44 (028) 90 24 30 74
Fax: +44 (028) 90 24 67 56
Email: reception@appletree.ie
Web: www.appletree.ie

Text © Lexy Higgins, 2006
Illustrations © Appletree Press, 2006
Illustrations by Stuart Wilkinson

A catalogue record for this book is available from the British Library.

'Where Do Balloons Go?'
and other poems by Lexy Higgins

ISBN-13: 978 0 86281 837 1
ISBN-10: 0 86281 837 0

Desk and Marketing Editor: Jean Brown
Editorial: Jim Black
Designer: Stuart Wilkinson
Production Manager: Paul McAvoy

9 8 7 6 5 4 3 2 1

AP3321

Contents

Dedication

I speak from the heart
As you can probably tell,
And I'd like to thank those
Who have loved me well:
I'll begin with my parents
Without whom I wouldn't be.
All of my life they have
Been there for me.
Along came Joe, we share wedded bliss.
Life without him, I truly would miss.
Next, my Eennie, the jewel in the crown.
The best thing on the planet
To wipe away a frown.
To my brothers Eddie, Patrick and Hugh.
My chance to say in print
How much I love you.
To Georgie and Moira –
Two sisters of mine –
I'd like to tell you
That you're simply devine!
You gave me the push I needed –
My very own book!
I've arrived, we've succeeded!

P.S. To Aunt Theresa: 'Thank you'

Where Do Balloons Go?

Where do balloons go?
I'd really like to know.
As they float high into the sky
My suspense begins to grow.
They may linger around a little
Or sail off very quick.
But how high can they really go?
It's a very special trick.
Do they hover above the clouds?
Do they see angels in the sky?
I suppose I'll never know that
Until the day I die.

Do balloons land on the moon?
Do they gather in outer space?
Is there a piece of sky somewhere, saying?
'Welcome to Balloons' Place!'
Balloons mean happy occasions.
They say let's celebrate,
They say hello or thank you
Or, yes that is the date.
So the next time you see a balloon
Floating on its way.
Stop and ask this question –
Where is he gliding to today?

Headin' for a Weddin'

I've been doin' a lot of thinking
'bout this an' 'bout that.
Should I buy a pair of dainty shoes,
or a fabulous fancy hat?
Perhaps I'll wear a crochet shawl
an' sashay about with ease.
I'll definitely not wear a flower –
it would only make me sneeze.

You see I'm headin' for a weddin',
an' I wanna look me best.
I don't want some oul doll sayin',
"Sure she's only half dressed."
I think I'll push the boat out
an' go for the whole hog.
I wanna look real glamorous,
not like an ugly oul frog.

I'll buy the best of gear
an' be the talk of the town.
Me family's right an' respectable,
I wouldn't want to let them down.
So if you're headin' for the weddin',
keep your eyes peeled for me.
Up the aisle, near the front –
the bride, that'll be me.

Peace

There is a large shop,
very close by me.
So I thought I'd take a trip there
to see what I could see.

I squeezed inside the head stand
hoping to buy a peaceful thought.
By the time I'd nudged past stress,
I found they had all been bought.
The assistant said, "the far side –
that's where they had been".
I leapt across – but all I found
was an ugly washing-machine.
So I wandered through the narrow stall,
known as the throat.
I had a little laugh there –
a frog sounding like a goat.

I edged into the main store, feeling very grand.
To my delight I quickly fell
upon the emotions stand.
Red hearts, satin and lace,
the emotions were scattered all over the place.
I lovingly gazed through them,
absorbing the display,
I decided on my purchase but to my dismay,
"Sorry dear," the assistant said.
"This sale is not to be,
For if you look inside that heart
you already have all three."

I studied the heart more carefully
and yes I could see –
Peace, love and happiness
inside that heart for me.

Donegal Here We Come

We all clambered inta two cars
An' we started out on our way.
We were all off to Donegal,
In the glorious month of May.
The journey had only begun
Already me patience were wearin' thin –
The state of his drivin',
Sure, it was an' awful sin.
Swayin' fast round corners
An' fixin' at his hair.
If he continued on like that,
I was gonna be like a bear!
Me wee one in the back, shoutin',
"I want a wee wee – drink."
Travellin' along the way, I began to think.
If I fell inta money an' became well off.
I cud send the family on ahead
An' arrive later like a toff!

Well anyway me thoughts broke,
As me ma, in the back,
She began to choke!
She coughed an' she spluttered
An' she wasn't getting any air,
But through it all she managed to say,
"Is my fegs anywhere near there?"
I rolled me eyes to the heavens
An' I said if there's anyone there,
Let me arrive in Donegal,
Before I pull out all me hair!
Me da he was in the other car.
Me sister had her eye on him.
Fer the way he was lukin' a late
He wasn't attendin' any gym.

The 'sat nav' on the windscreen
Told us our destination was on the right.
We'd all made excellent time,
An' arrived before the night.
We approached the hotel together
Our holiday had begun.

All hyped up an' excited
An' getting ready for some fun.
We had our meal an' sung some songs,
While the kids they danced an' played.
The first day had ended
So we headed off to bed.

Next morning at breakfast
The teasin' it began.
That'll be me brother-in-law
Sure he's a terrible man.
Me ma an' da sat at the top
They enjoyed the banter.
Straight away after breakfast,
We all headed fer a canter.
We squeezed in some bowls
An' a little bit a shoppin'.
The kids, they played 'Gameboys'
Then racin' an' hoppin'.

We ate at the 'Yellow Pepper',
The food it was mighty tasty.
We lingered round the restaurant,
No need to be hasty.
Back to the 'Silver Tassie',
Our nightly sing song to complete.
Each tryin' to out sing the other
Without wantin' to compete.
The vacation was a huge success –
We were all still friends.
Well, with exception of me an' me husband
An' me an' the other ten!

Comfort

I've had days
When I could see warm light,
Folding about me and cuddling tight.
I felt free, airy and light.
Please grant me peace,
Today and tonight.

Devils In Disguise!

Let us imagine two little girls,
We'll name them Aoife and Katie-Do.
They get up to mischievious things you know,
They are not little angels – these two!

Picture two angelic children
One blonde and blue,
The other auburn with big brown eyes-
They'd win you over too.

One day, when their mummy
had washing on the line,
She smiled quietly to herself
because her clothes were drying fine.

But later when she checked again –
She put her hand to her head
For somehow, someone had
painted the clothes all red!

She turned to her two little darlings and asked,
"Did you see anything?"
But the two little devils in disguise–
they hadn't saw a thing!

Later in the afternoon,
while mum was busy making their lunch,
She thought she heard a Biff! Bang! Buff!
That sounded like a punch.

She opened the toy room door.
There standing before her eyes,
Two little devils all black and blue
But this time without their disguise!

Ciggs

Suck in,
Puff out,
Could someone tell me
What it's all about?
Smoky clothes, smelly rooms.
Am I wise inhaling these fumes?
Time to stop –
Wait an' see.
"I don't smoke!"
That'll be me.

The Shopkeeper

A wee shop in County Down,
Almost shut – hardly making a pound.
That's what you think, before opening the door.
Then there it all is, stock, ceiling to floor.
Behind the worn counter he stood, larger than life.
His stature was tall – he'd make two of his wife –
The gentle giant, with the kind soft heart,
It's terribly sad he and Maggie must part.

Big Bears

I sat on a step and said my prayers.
For the wood beside was full of bears!
I crept behind a tree to sneak.
Craftily, I began to peak.
Bears of sizes large and small
Playing with a round beach ball.
My eyes they quickly opened wide
As a huge brown bear had saw me hide!
Close up to me he rapidly came
And playfully asked: "Would you like a game?"

Normal Days

The strain of pain.
We hope in vain,
For ease and peace of mind.
Shoulders ache, back does break,
A neck that crunches and grinds.

Weeks goes by,
Still we try,
To tread and work and be normal.
A little brush, a little dust –
Housework, nothing formal.

Head is fine!
If you forget the time,
I couldn't remember names.
Then you see, it's not just me.
These are just life's little games.

Hope

Tiny
Trickles.
Slip, slap, slop,
Is how the rain sounds
Parachuting gently
Before it hits the ground.
Another day is ending
As quickly as before.
I hope that I can sleep soon
And hear the rain no more!

Just Jones

I'd drove up from the country
An' I was frightened of getting lost,
I tuk a right turn here an' a left turn there
An' I kept me fingers crossed.

I arrived safely in the city
An' pulled up outside the B.B.C.
I was sure an' certain those slickers
Were looking at me.

So yer man behind the desk
He gave me a badge an' pin
I was standin' there
Looking all La-de-da at him.

"It's the *Just Jones* show I'm appearin' on.
Which way do I go?
Well with an accent like that Love –
I really do not know!

But interviewees for George,
They all go up that lift.
An' you needn't luk at me like that Love –
You're definitely no gift!"

Ma nose was in the air
as I headed on me way.
I wasn't gonna let the like of thon –
ruin me special day.

Oh the excitement was chokin' me
as I waited to begin,
The silence it was deafenin',
ya cudda heard a pin!

I was parked up on the 'Just Jones Show',
Smiling like the cat that got the cream.
I had to pinch meself now an' then
For I thought it might be a dream!

I enjoyed telling me pieces,
An' sure the time it flew.
Me wee stint on the radio,
It was over before I knew.

But me day out to the city
An' me five minutes of fame.
Gave me such a buzz inside,
There, marked permanently on me brain.

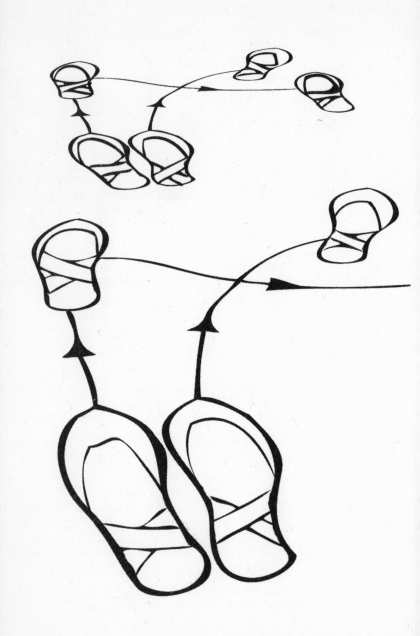

Tiptoe

My dancing teacher said to me,
Point your toe and hop, two three.
This I did but to my dismay,
These are the words I heard her say:
"NO! NO! NO! NO! NO!"

"High up on your tiptoe,
Point and hop and flow and flow."
I gritted my teeth, pointed my toe
Hop two three and here I go.
"NO! NO! NO! NO! NO!"

"Back to the beginning," I heard her wail.
"You're as graceful as a slimy snail.
Look! Point and hop and back two three,
Stay close behind and follow me.
NO! NO! NO! NO! NO!"

Years of practice did I do,
Holes in more than just one shoe…
My dancing teacher said to me,
"Point your toe and hop two three."
I lifted my chin, pointed my toe.
Waited for the beat, then off I go!
Finished my dance went back to line.
Hoping I had danced in time.

My dancing teacher said to me,
Clapping her hands
and smiling with glee
"This is a dance you
KNOW! KNOW! KNOW! KNOW! KNOW!"

Graceful Losers

Sandcastles to build.
Will you lend me a hand?
Hurry sweetheart
Get me more sand!
It's a competition,
So…
Let's do our best
To beat the opposition.
Our little palace is finished.
Rocks and seaweed too.
Oh it's not just about winning,
It's about *living* too.

Moanin' Minnie

Let me tell ya a bit about meself
An' see if you can understand me.
I take these excruciating pains, *there*,
In me back an' on down into me knee.

I took a stoon-in' pain in the back of me head,
Sure if they hadn't a found me, I'd be lyin' there
dead!
They think I'm jokin' when I say pain.
Well listen to this, ay, an' listen again.

Now does that sound like a heart beat,
or a lambeg drum?
Well between it an' the ringin' in me ears,
I feel the need to hum.
Oh me elbow! Did you hear that crack?
Oh no not again! It's me back, me back!

Last week I called with me doctor,
says I, "I'm really bad."
Says he, "Minnie you'd better be
or I'll be awfully mad.
You were with me only yesterday
and twice the day before.
You're givin' me double vision…
I can't take this anymore!"

I don't complain much,
sure ya wouldn't hear a word.
Normally I'm as chirper as any oul bird.
They call me 'Moanin' Minnie',
an' I don't know why.
Sure I'll just suffer here in silence,
'till the day I die.

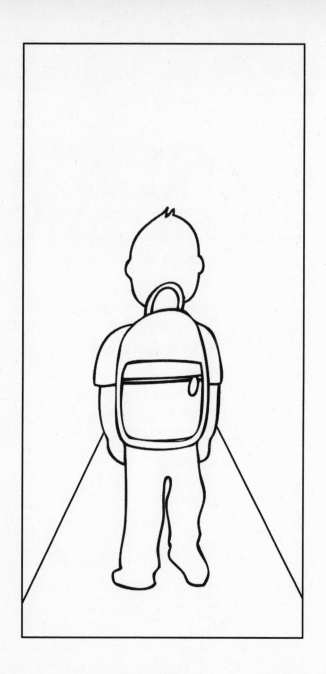

School Eve

How do I feel today my love?
Oh, how do I feel today?
I watch you play my sweetheart
My heart might snap in two,
Tomorrow is that special day
That you trip off to school.

We spent many days together,
Just you and I.
So I suppose it's natural for me
To lament and cry.

The big wide world awaits you –
I must edge back – you see,
This, my little sweetheart
Is difficult for me.

I'll feel your every movement
I'll still be your backbone,
Even though you're at school,
And I'll be here at home.

So go with love my darling
Enjoy your new school days.
I'll be thinking of you
In oh so many ways.

My Friend Judy

I've this friend called Judy, I saw the other day.
I noticed very quickly
She was walkin' in a weird way.
You know those clowns you see
With red noses and big feet?
Well, I hate to be the one ta say
Compared ta Judy, their feet were neat.
I didn't want to offend her so I caged around the
block.
"Your tracksuit's cool," I said. "Is that new socks?"
They're certainly new trainers
You haven't worn them before,
Cause you're still in this room
But your feet are out the door!
I know they were cheap and cheerful,
But wearing shoes like that, Judy,
Will only make you tearful.
So stop walkin' like a frogman
An' take your bargain to the bin.
Or give them to the charity shop
In their window they'd put in
Two oars and a bright yellow sign,
To get the buyers interested in the new design.
'Shoes for sale in the shape of a canoe.
BUY ONE – YOU GET THE TWO!'

The Dentist's Drill

I was sitting in me dentist's room
Where I heard me dentist drill.
The dread it took a hold of me,
He was pulling teeth at will!
I started to shake an' shiver,
Me turn was soon to come,
The injection was takin' effect
An' me gum was getting numb.

The assistant's heels I could hear
Clippin' on the tiles.
She looked at me from the corridor
All teeth an' all smiles.
A little nod of her head
An' a flicker of her eye,
My turn to face the dentist's drill.
Why, oh why, oh why?

I slowly slugged to the leather chair
Sat back an' threw up me feet.
I began to get that sinkin' feelin' ya get
When ya know that you've been beat.
I lay an' looked at the ceilin' an'
Waited for me dentist to come,
The fear was wellin' inside me an'
I was cryin' in me heart for me Mum.

He came in an' hovered above me
Like an eagle stalkin' its prey.
I was looking right up his nose then
An' it put me right off me tay.
Me mouth was full of fingers
And open as wide as could be.
How did he expect me to answer
All those questions he was askin' me?

"This one's to come out," he tells me.
"Ah, your mouth is a disgrace.
Open nice an' wide now,
Till I take off your brace."
He removed the brace an' pulled the tooth
I didn't feel any pain –
But believe me when I tell you
I'm in no hurry back again.

I stood up from the chair
An' dusted meself down,
An' I took a long look at him,
Standin' there in his clean white gown.
I gave a little smile, me mouth all tilted to one side
But it was me genuine feelings
I was tryin' hard to hide.
He'd just hammered me an' battered me
an' ridiculed me to the nurse,
But now he was really goin' to hurt me –
by emptying me purse!

Butter Him Up

The Easter season had arrived,
I began to take an itch,
Fer a holiday or a trip away,
So I began to make me pitch.

Me husband was in the garden,
So I waited fer a while.
I had to tread, real carefully,
Or me plan cud fall in a pile!

I made him tatty bread an' soda
Bacon an' egg on the side.
Ah, the way I laid the table,
I was burstin,' full of pride.

"Come inta the house me darlin',
Take the weight off yer feet.
Settle down at the table dear,
Cool down – in out of the heat.

Would ya like another egg dear,
Perhaps another slice of bacon?
Sure you're working hard all day dear,
I'm sure your feet are achin'.

Come over here me darlin'–
Til' I give ye a hug.
A wee drop more tay dear?
Just hold up yer mug.

Did you say ya wanted a holiday?
Now, why didn't I think a that?
Sit down here on the sofa dear,
Away from that dirty oul cat.

Oh, you didn't *say* holiday,
Perhaps I was mistaken.
But you're right dear anyway,
Let's try to squeeze a break in!"

Lazy Day

Let's have a lazy day!
Do you really think we should?
Lazing in our jammys –
Will it do us any good?

Let's stuff ourselves with sweeties,
Let's not brush our teeth or hair.
Let's slouch around the house today
Like we simply just don't care.

Let's make the most of our time.
Let's cuddle up close and tight
And if we stay in jammys today
We won't have to change tonight.

Mourne Men

Have ya heard about the Mourne men?
Well, let me tell you it's all true.
They'd wine ya an' dine ya
An' make a princess out of you.
They'd treat ya like a treasure
They'd cradle ya like a tot.
They'd shower ya with affection
Whether you're interested or not.

Now some of them love themselves,
More than they love their women.
Some of them pose around the pool
While others go swimming.
Some strut like a peacock
Others are bandy like a hen.
But you'll travel far afield
Ta beat the bold Mourne men!

Elastic Band

Tight, tight elastic band,
Someone take me by the hand.
Release this pressure, release this strain.
Someone help me live again.

Life is out there – I know it's true.
Why can I not see this through?
What is this demon I possess
Shielding me from happiness?

My thoughts are deep.
I want to sleep.
Sleep. Sleep. Sleep.
Ease this pressure.
Stop this pain
Pull myself together again.

Fair an' Square

As I wandered round the supermarket,
I heard this squealing voice shout:
"Move ta the next aisle I tell ya,
Or I'll have ta knock ya out!
Get out of me road, I tell ya,
Or I'll hit ya with this loaf.
Move your trolley Mrs,
Or I'll have ta kill us both!"

I ran ta the top and I peaked down the aisle,
An' me mouth it opened as wide as a mile.
Fer me eyes were sayin' one thing
While me brain was sayin' another.
But there was no mistakin' him,
It was my wee brother!
Standin' there – punchin' the air –
Half-cooked – out of his scone!
Fightin' the *Green Giant* board –
Ach, his marbles had all gone!

I pushed me trolley forward.
An' says I, "Brother dear.
You've won that fight fair an' square,
Now – get yourself outta here!"

Eennie

Precious petal.
Perfect poise,
Gurgling such wonderful noise.
Delightful darling,
Dainty dame,
Eennie Smyth Higgins
That's her name.

Godzilla

Where's the genius who invented make-up?
I'd love ta shake his hand.
Cos when I wake up in the morning,
I'm like a creature from another land!

I force me eyes open at day break,
Me mouth cud be stuck to the pilla.
Me hair is like a hedgehog, standin'
An' I feel like a weepin' willa.

Then into me own little salon I go.
Ta begin me daily task,
Ta try an' transform the alien,
Into a beautifully formed mask!

The shower it hits me body
An' I awaken in a flash.
I have to be at work fer nine
So I'll have to make a dash.

I begin the slow process
An' it takes about an' hour.
Ta transform me from Godzilla
Inta a fabulous flower!

Beehive

Fear that fills your being,
Fear that fills your heart,
Fear that looms inside your head
And pulls your world apart.

The stomach knots and churns,
The fire of fear that burns.
You're choking on your air
You take each breath in turns.

Such a suffocating feeling,
Like drowning whilst alive.
Your skin may crawl and itch
Like living in a beehive.

Life

A family tree
It seems to me,
Is strange,
Yet so inventive.
That some should die,
So some shall live,
Is really quite
Dementive!

Diamond Dilemma

The jeweller's shop was sparkling bright,
As we strolled through the glass door.
The price tags on them diamonds –
He nearly fell ta the floor.
He'd came in ta buy me a diamond,
No half measures mind.
An' honest to goodness diamond –
The expensive film star kind!

There was solitaires an' clusters,
Squares and triangles too.
Which one would he go fer, I wondered?
Ohh! Maybe I'd get two!
I loitered round the earrings
To let him have some time.
He had a difficult decision –
Which diamond would be mine?

He handed me the titchy wee box –
I gave him a sloppy big kiss!
I could barely contain meself,
I'd waited a lifetime on this!
When I looked at it – when I found it!
A hint of a glimmer from the ice.
I stared at it – an' I glared at him
An' said, "It's awfully – nice!"

I sat down at the table
An' I began me thanks,
Fer my teeny, weeny diamond
An' me massive shank!

Free Fallin'

Ya talk about being up the creek,
without a paddle,
Or ridin' a wild pony,
without a saddle.
That's just how I feel,
I'm free fallin' off a cliff
Ma heart it's poundin' like mad
An' me head it's ready to lift.
Now you're probably all wonderin',
What could be that bad?
That she's goin' astray in the head
An' nearly half-mad?

Well the truth is very simple
An' I suppose it cud be worse,
Three young hooligans,
They ran off with me purse.
Now there wasn't that much in it –
Two twenties an' a ten –
But the thought of my wee purse,
I'll never see it again!
It had sentimental value
it was givin' to me by a friend
An' the way my heart feels today,
it might never mend.

I hate to lose anything –
I'd rather give it away
Or in the case of the money,
save it for a rainy day.
But I'll have to get on with it
and remember life can be sunny.
Sure at the end of the day,
it's only oul money.

London Sights

We rode a red bus round London.
The sights were mighty fine.
We wandered up the West End,
To watch Mary Poppins step in time.

We clambered the steps at St Pauls!
We spied jewels in the grand Tower.
An' we queued to get on the London Eye,
Fer more than an hour!

London's Bridge wasn't fallin' down.
In fact, it looked pretty healthy.
As did Buckingham Palace,
The home of royalty an' wealthy.

We were gob-smacked at Big Ben!
We called at Madame Tussauds
An' Number Ten too.
The only thing we didn't manage,
Was a visit to the local zoo!

Fairies and Pixies

Fairies fly and pixies prance.
Together they make
A magical dance.
In and out the fairy ring,
The pixies laugh
And gleefully sing.
The pixie party has begun!
The fairies fly about the sun!
But, in a twinkling,
When the children play around
The pixies and fairies –
They don't make a sound!

The Double of Me Ma

"Who's she like?"
I heard her say,
As she tuk another
Swig of her tay.

"She's like her da,
There round the chin.
Ach, my goodness –
Sure she's the picture of him!"

I weaked me breeches up
An' I gave a little sigh,
Before I said slowly:
Have ye something in yer eye?

It's my wee mammy
I'm the double of –
Sure listen carefully
I even have her cough.

Me eyes are as big as saucers,
Me mouth has a cupid's bow.
An' just like my wee Mammy,
I've a bunion on me toe!

Ball of Blue

My princess handed me a flower.
A cornflower she had plucked.
A little ball of blue,
Without any stalk.
No stem to put into water,
No stem to help it live.

A more precious gift,
My princess could not have give!
I pressed that little cornflower,
I pressed it to my heart.
This symbol of affection
From my mind will never part.

Withheld Information

A letter arrived in the post today.
I opened it like any other.
I read the first two lines
And couldn't read another.

There in bold print,
There in black and white.
Information to make me smile
And fill me with delight!

It began – 'Dear Madam,'
It ended – 'With Kind Regards.'
The information in the middle?
Well, that's business of ours!

Lion or Mouse

If you're feeling terrified –
Like a tiny, timid mouse –
Bring some lion vibes inside
And come out of your little mouse house.

Be fearless and courageous.
Don't crumple up and hide.
Be confident and daring
And have a little pride.

Prepare early in the morning.
Think beautiful thoughts and then,
If the mouse gradually creeps in
You can roar him out again.

Don't hold your head into your chest –
Don't be quiet or shy.
Always slant your chin up
And hold your shoulders high.

Remember! You're a winner!
Don't ever have any doubt.
Let me hear the little mouse squeak:
"Who let the lion out?"

Uncle

My Uncle Dessie says to me, 'M.O.T.'
This may mean little to you,
But it means the world to me.
M.O.T. could mean 'I'm well'
Or 'How are you today?'
M.O.T. could be 'Hello',
Or 'Thank you for your stay'.
So Uncle – as promised –
A poem for you, from me:
Best of luck, my darling Uncle,
And Happy M.O.T.

Dedicated to my uncle who had a stroke

Ragged Ears

When you read a novel's last page,
That's it, it's read! It's done!
But a little book of poetry
The end might never come!
It could give you hours of enjoyment –
It may fill you with laughter or tears.
A truly loved poetry book
Is the one with the ragged ears!

Index to First Lines